Cyberpsychology

Mind and Internet Relationship

Juan Moisés de la Serna

Translated by Sebastian Bolivar

Tektime editorial

2019

"Cyberpsychology: Mind and Internet Relationship"

Written by Juan Moisés de la Serna

Translated by Sebastian Bolivar

First Edition: December of 2015

Current Edition: November of 2019

© Juan Moisés de la Serna, 2019

© Tektime editions, 2019

All rights reserved

Distributed by Tektime

https://www.traduzionelibri.it

PREFACE

This book addresses a new branch in psychology called Cyberpsychology, which shows how there has been a change in the person-technology relationship, analyzing how new developments affect the day-to-day life of a person, as well as the mental health of its users. All this backed by an extensive bibliography on the latest research conducted in this area.

Social networks, the Internet and all the technological advances of recent years have changed the way we see the world and behave, a change in many cases radical, which cannot go unnoticed to Psychology majors, the science that studies human behavior.

The invention and use of tools such as the hatchet or the needle, first, and then machines such as the car or the computer, have subsequently revolutionized the way of relating to oneself and others.

To speak with a family member or a friend it is as simple as connecting persons that wish to communicate via Skype regardless of location. The technological advances that happened in this last decades has been so fast that it forced people to adapt so they can take advantage of this evolving technology. In this book it addresses how change has been produced and how it affects the day- to-day developments of the person just as in the mental health of its users. All this endorsed by an extensive bibliography about the latest studies conducted on this scope.

Objective:

The objective of the book will serve as a first approach to the up and coming branch of psychology known as Cyberpsychology.

So, it treats the most relevant topics offering results of the latest studies conducted this past two years across the globe about this subject.

All this explained with simple and easy to read language, away from technical terms explaining each concept so it can truly work as an initiation guide.

Addressee:

- Professionals in health that have to confront a more complex clinics because of provoked cases that addresses the use and abuse of the internet and new technologies.

- Professors that are trying to be up to date about the changes they observe in their students.

- A worried father about the benefits and prejudice that new technologies might have on the lives of their children.

- To any person that is interested in knowing how technology is influencing in modern society, transforming the way which it relates.

Theme

Up next, every main chapter of this work will be themed:

- The Risks of the Internet: Where we analyze every new phenomena, syndrome and disorder related with technology, that every day it becomes more present inside clinics.

- Network Opportunities: Tackling how it changes social relationships, and especially work relationships and how we have to be prepared for it.

- Digital Identity and Virtual Words: Where we approach how we interact in a virtual world, that sometimes we can see as a stranger the people that we know, but where they don't behave as they do in the real world, all this presented from the perspective of the latest results from obtained studies all around the world.

- The Psychology of Social Networks: The most popular networks such as Facebook and Twitter, have been the source of information that are starting to be analyzed by investigators in this section where we offer the first results of this novel studies.

- Psychotechnology: Where we design and implement new tools orientated to improve the diagnostic as well as the treatment of different psychopathologies. Where we include the use of robotics and online therapy among others.

ACKNOWLEDGMENT

I will take advantage of the situation and begin to express my gratitude to all the people that collaborated with their contribution to the realization of this text, especially to Dr. David Lavilla Muñoz, Professor of Digital Communication and new Tendencies of the European University and to Dr. Daniela Galindo Bermúdez, President of, "Talking with Julis": The solution for communication and apprenticeship of people with disabilities.

We have technology, that will help us prevail,
But let's be careful, that we might fail.

Sometimes we are there, when we are connected
But we think not of ourselves, when the keyboard rejected.

Fantasies we transmit, as they cannot see
To others we tell, what we believe to be.

Limits are there to be, as we assure
Technology, won't oppress thy be.

Uncontrolled hours, won't let us eat
Always hooked, we shall not be.

LOVE.

Dedicated to My Parents

Index

CHAPTER 1. CYBERPSYCHOLOGY: THE NEW PSYCHOLOGY

Cyberpsychology is one of the newest branches in psychology that emerged from the necessity of understanding how technology affects individuals and how they change in function of more or less extensive use of new developments.

While in many universities' no such program exists, it is undeniable the necessity to analyze and comprehend human behavior when we use technology, either for leisure or for work.

Cyberpsychology therefore incorporates the technological element as the central axis of its analysis, without losing site that the person is the one interacting one way or another. Describe and comprehend the habits, use and misuse of that technology have been the object of study of Cyberpsychology.

We have to take into account that, with neurosciences, they are the psychology branches that change the most, since both of them allow to offer a better understanding as instruments of evaluation and observations are each time much keener and enable details that beforehand were indispensable.

A lot has been said about the negative effects Internet use has in maintaining healthy social relationships, but is it like this on all cases?

The technological mediums as a computer or smartphones allow friends, acquaintances and old school buddies to be connected thanks to digital applications such as Facebook, in this world every day more globalized.

But now it has been considered that an excessive use of one's hours with this or any other leisure driven activities such as watching television or listening to music encourages social isolation and it would favor the apparition of depression.

Other studies considered that the consequences of a depressed state have a previous origin that have much more to do then just isolating one's self and avoiding human contact with what a computer screen or a cellphone gives you.

Something that might seem contradictory with new results and with the idea that communication mediums such as the Internet is that allows more connections and not isolation, then, how can someone isolate themselves from the world being connected via social networks with so much people on the other side of the screen? To resolve this question a study has been carried out by the New England University (Australia) whose results have been published on the scientific magazine Open Journal of Depression.

In it were forty-one teenagers evaluated on two separate occasions with a year separation where we implemented various measures to examine both mood and use of social networks through the Internet where they had in mind not just the time invested but also the quality of their communication.

The results in spite of supporting a depressed state of mind and massive use of communication mediums through the Internet, established that this type of relationship is a positive type. That said, people will find necessary support with the ones they interact to overcome their negative personal situations, converting so in a tool of depression prevention.

The difference with the previous results can be that in this study they do not take to account just the number of daily hours invested on massive communication, it has been proven to be related with people that have depression tendencies and even so this can be determined to an addiction problem to new technology, but also the quality of it has been evaluated, that is to say, where interaction happens with significant persons that help serve the model for example, or to simply know how to listen and support when it is needed, it is enough to help people to not fall into depression.

Despite the small number of study participants, the conclusions seem to explain the contradictory of the previous results by introducing a new factor not taken into account so far, the quality of communication, this being the determinant for the technology-mental health relationship to be positive or not.

Below is a series of research on what is currently being studied in this area and what conclusions have been drawn so far. For this, the results are presented grouped according to their theme and study, the virtual world with its avatars and the most used social networks, such as Facebook or Twitter; and the specific software for neurorehabilitation.

There are many demands that this young branch of psychology receives, in order to answer the questions that health professionals and even parents raise, such as, for example, what risks does technology entail in the youngest?

CHAPTER 2. THE RISKS OF THE INTERNET

One of the greatest concerns of parents is regarding the correct handling of new technologies by minors. Everyone can understand that technology offers great benefits, especially in the workplace, and even at home. Houses can have a washing machines, microwaves, electric cookers, all of the important devices and technologies that save up time that previously would take up a good part of the day.

On the other hand, in the house there are other devices oriented almost exclusively to leisure, for example, television, radio or computers. Removing the educational and learning process that can be used of them, for example, follow a language course through CDs, watch TV documentaries or prepare homework with the computer. Apart from that, parents always have doubts about the consequences in children of these leisure-oriented devices.

Although pediatricians, child psychologists and educators already said it, and this was corroborated by some research in this regard of the Public Health England report, leaves no doubt about the harmful influence of television on children's health.

The report includes a study carried out in which forty-two thousand English minors participated, aged between 8 and 15 years, analyzing the harmful consequences of excessive hours in front of a television, whose conclusions leave no doubt, informing that those who spend more time are those who obtain a greater deficiency in academic results obtained by these, and attributes a direct relationship to the misuse of hours in front of the television with low self-esteem and with consequences of the their psyche like depression and anxiety.

Despite the benefits that can be attributed by providing information and entertainment, when the time spent on television exceeds four hours a day, there will also be a withdrawal in other activities, whether academic or recreational, thereby facilitating the isolation of your social media.

While it is true, that the report presented does not establish a cause-effect relationship leaving open to new research, discovering how this influence occurs, being among the possible explanations that, the longer one stays in front of a TV, the less time they will dedicate to social interaction with peers.

As time is limited, for both children and adults, when we spend a good part of the day watching television programs, we are necessarily neglecting other activities that we could develop.

In childhood, social relationships are important, since they serve to configure people, while developing communication skills and their identity is formed through comparison with others and belonging to a group of peers.

The cultivation of friendship is a fundamental activity at this stage of life, which requires a lot of time and is reduced to the extent that this time is devoted to watching television even if it is to watch educational programs.

The isolation and lack of establishment of relationships of fellowship and friendship with all the experiences that this entails, both positive and negative could be behind why these children have lower levels of self-esteem, since they are not developing interaction skills that others at their age already manage them perfectly.

Perhaps the most worrying part of this report is that a relationship has been observed between time in front of television and certain psychological pathologies. While it is true, that certain behaviors such as sedentary lifestyle and poor diet had previously been linked to health problems such as obesity, and in some cases, the onset of early diabetes. Related that in principle can affect anyone regardless of their age, but it is especially worrying when it occurs to minors.

Major Depression or Anxiety Disorders are the most serious consequences on the child's psychological health that are reported in this study, by spending too much time isolated in front of the television or computer screen.

With what is going to be configuring a clinical picture of consequences, both physical and psychological around the child that will drag during adulthood, if he/she or his/her parents do not put the necessary means to overcome this situation.

Once the conclusions of the report presented by Public Health England are known, it is only necessary to reflect on the role of parents or caregivers when leaving the child alone in front of the television, knowing that after four hours of watching it, the child will be more likely to suffer from low self-esteem, and over time will be more exposed to depression and anxiety disorders, clinical conditions that will require in the future of appropriate treatment by the specialist.

Cyberaddiction:

But the health dangers these young consumers do not remain there, and although technology is a tool and as such depends on the use or misuse, we give it, it may have greater influence on life and relationships.

Currently, it is difficult to find a student who does not routinely use the Internet for their work or leisure, so they may suffer from Internet addiction.

Each time the incursion of new technologies is carried out at an earlier age, practically from the first years of life, children now have touchpads and with a few more years have their own Smartphones with Internet access.

Today, even in schools, the use of new technologies is encouraged, through touchpads instead of books, in addition to the teacher using his/her electronic board all connected to the Internet where specific consultation materials are designed for classes.

But when you start with the Internet, there is no limitation in its use, especially when you go into games or social networks, an activity that increasingly requires more time, until you without knowing, developed an addiction.

One of the most prominent risks in this area is that of technology addiction, since it must be borne in mind that any human substance or activity can become addictive provided that the following conditions exist:

- Loss of control of will.

- Use of excessive time in this activity by removing it from others, whether labor or social relations.

- Certain level of isolation, unless they are "social addictions"

- With negative consequences both economic, emotional and family, due to such dependence.

- With "inclusions" of thoughts, making it difficult not to think about it, and causing an elevation of anxiety and restlessness when you are without access to such addiction.

- With negative consequences on academic performance.

- In some cases, it also entails some personal neglect that can be shown in lack of hygiene.

All this explained by the same neuronal mechanisms that allows to tend to repeated behaviors, given for its pleasant and positive consequences thus facilitating learning.

It also happens with the use of new technologies, which, if they cease to be useful for work or daily life, and become "necessary" or "essential", may be giving rise to a technological addiction, either to the "excessive" use of new terminals, Smartphone or touchpads, as well as the intensive and "uncontrolled" use of instant messaging services, such as Messenger, WhatsApp, Twitter or Tuenti.

This has caused the emergence of novel phenomena that did not exist before, so they have had to create new terms to contemplate it, as is the case of the F.O.M.O. (Fear Of Missing Out), or fear of missing out on the latest, that is, the need to be aware of social networks at all times so as not to miss the last mobile device that has come out or the last video of your favorite singer, identified by the University of Essex (England) together with the University of California and the University of Rochester (USA) published in the scientific journal Computer in Human Behavior.

For its part, Villanova University (USA) has described for the first time a new phenomenon called "Sleep Texting", which refers to the phenomenon of not having a regular sleep, as there are constant interruptions to read messages and send new ones. This phenomenon accounts for a decrease in the quantity and quality of sleep among young people, who are the main users who suffer from it.

In this sense it has been carried out by a study by the University of Washington and Lee University (USA) whose results have been published in the scientific journal Psychology of Popular Media Culture.

It analyzes the influence of the use of M.S.N. (acronym in English for text messages) in the health of university students. Eighty-three students participated in this study, where health quality was analyzed using the Pittsburgh Sleep Quality Index, which provides information on three indices: exhaustion, sleep problems and social relationships.

We wanted to study the effect on these three indices based on the number of messages that were received and sent during the day, finding that the three indices were negatively affected as the number of messages that had to "manage" grew, but where the greatest effects were found with respect to sleep problems, where starting from "moderate" levels of messages were already beginning to cause high levels of anxiety and thus difficulties in falling asleep.

The lower quantity and quality of sleep will have consequences in "day life", with a lower retention capacity and attention among students, and if this situation is maintained over time, it can even affect health.

Hence the importance of "educating" the youngest in the use of these electronic devices, since as indicated, these can generate problems of performance and concentration, in addition to affecting social relations and the most serious of all, It can affect your health, due to the maintenance of high levels of stress and lack of quality sleep.

And all this assuming that the person is "owner of his/her will", that is, that he/she has not yet fallen into a technological addiction, which would have even greater negative effects. The main problem of detecting these types of situations is that parents do not know how to assess to what extent it is something "normal" or has already passed the line of appropriateness and has become unhealthy.

Likewise, the person who suffers it, despite realizing the difficulties and harmful consequences that it entails, is unable to recognize that they have a problem and that they need help from others to overcome it, even that they may need a specialist to overcome their addiction.

As can be seen in the previous result, technology can cause serious difficulties in the day-to-day life of the person, both that can put their health at risk, as in the case of damaging the quality and quantity of sleep due to having to answer message that they receive.

Today it is difficult to think that a young man does not own an account on Facebook, Twitter or Tuenti among others, since they were born in the era of social networks, considering themselves as "digital natives", that is, those who were born after the decade of the eighties and that they always had access to this new technologies.

Those who have a few more years, those who were born before the 80s, have to make an effort to stay informed and trained with this of social networks, and that is what is called "digital immigrants", that is, people who were born without these possibilities and now they have to enter this world, sometimes confusing and sometimes disconcerting, but in any case useful and necessary.

Just as previously it was requested for some jobs to have a driver's license and a minimum educational level, now it is required that candidates have sufficient skills in handling computers and social networks. Following these new tools, unthinkable jobs have emerged a few years ago, such as Community Manager, responsible for forums and virtual communities, or the most technical ones responsible for promoting websites such as S.E.O. and S.E.M., which seek to achieve greater visibility in the social networks and on the Internet of a particular brand or company.

For their part, young people have been incorporating the tools offered by this new technology in their life, both academic and leisure, there are already many universities that partially or totally teach their teachings online, being able to connect from any fixed or mobile device, such as touchpads, iPads, or smartphones.

Teachers having a double function, that of organizing and recording the classes to be taught and that of virtual tutoring to solve the doubts that may have arisen from them.

This has made it possible to open the doors of universities to students from all over the world, with the only requirement that they have the necessary linguistic skills to follow the classes, and yes, a device with an Internet connection.

In this regard, the only thing that has not been solved has been at the time of the exams, which are required to be face-to-face, either at the university itself or at a center arranged in the student's country.

So that it is true that the student who is taking the exam properly knows the subject of the exam.

In my particular case, after taking several years teaching face-to-face in different universities, I had to do a training course to continue with my work as a teacher, but this time through social networks, for which I had to adapt the technological tools that previously used the new demands, including the familiarization of training platforms such as Moodle, or the use of videoconferencing programs to teach on-line teaching, which allowed me to teach classes in Spain, both in the Peninsula and in the Islands, while being followed from Latin America.

But there are Internet risks that arise when youth leisure becomes almost exclusive in the intensive use of this technology, losing social contact and sometimes, contact with reality itself. There are many studies that are being done in this regard, following this new modality where new cases of cyberadicts are detected every day, that is, people who are unable to disconnect from the network, facilitating social isolation, and neglect of mental and personal hygiene, also associated with improper nutrition, all these Internet risks caused by an inadequate education on the correct use of technology.

A new study has been carried out by Kaohsiung

Medical University and Hsiao-Kang Hospital (Taiwan), the results of which have been published in the scientific journal J.A.M.A. Pediatrics where two thousand two hundred and ninety-three young people have been followed for 2 years, evaluated at 6, 12 and 24 months.

The objective of this study was to find the new and predictable factors of addictions to new technologies, for which the level of addiction was evaluated through the standardized scale called C.I.A.S. (Chen Internet Addiction Scale), in addition to depression levels through the Chinese version of C.E.S.-D. (Center for Epidemiological Studies Depression Scale), the attention deficit hyperactivity disorder assessed by the A.D.H.D.S. (Attention-Deficit / Hyperactivity Disorder Self-rated Scale), the social phobia through the F.N.E. (Fear of Negative Evaluation Scale) and the hostility of the participants through the B.D.H.I.C.-S.F. (Buss-Durkee Hostility Inventory – Chinese Version – Short Form).

The results inform that those young men who had high levels of hostility showed higher levels of addiction after 2 years, thus becoming the best source of this psychopathology. In contrast, the adolescents who participated in the study showed that the best source of future addiction is related to suffering from attention deficit hyperactivity disorder.

In both boys and girls, previous levels of social phobia or depression were not relevant when predicting future addiction to technologies. The study also offers a "revealing" fact that, in just 2 years, more than 10% of the participants were affected by Internet addiction, the difference in the number of cases among the "addicts" being insignificant male and female.

Hence the importance of these studies, which show the risks of the Internet in young people. Studies necessary to be able to create specific programs to prevent it with special emphasis on education, as a determining factor of self-regulation in the management of new technologies, that is, with proper education it is expected that the young person will be able to properly use the technology and don't misuse it.

In addition to the above, and in the specific case of young people, this technological education must be accompanied by an intervention program regarding the correct management of hostility, and in young women in the diagnosis and treatment of attention deficit disorder with hyperactivity, thereby avoiding future complications of Internet addiction.

Young people may be exposed to this cyberaddiction, the next thing we should know would be, is it possible to detect Internet addiction in young people?

This is precisely what they try to analyze from Payam Noor University (Iran) whose results have been published in the International Journal of Behavioral Research & Psychology.

The study involved three hundred and eighty students, one hundred ninety-four girls and the rest boys, all of them attending the institute.

Three objects of study were raised, the first, to determine the extent to which young students suffer from Internet addiction, the second, to verify whether this presence of addiction is related to the level of sincerity expressed within the family, and finally if gender differences exist in the previous two.

For this, the standardized questionnaire I.A.T. (Internet Addiction Test) to assess the level of Internet addiction of young people, and one created for that purpose to assess the level of sincerity at home of the participants.

The results report that boys experience significantly a higher level of Internet addiction than girls.

Likewise, the level of lack of intrafamily sincerity increases to the extent that Internet dependence does, and therefore it is expressed significantly more in boys compared to girls.

So, it is possible to detect addiction among children simply by observing their level of sincerity in the family, when they start looking for excuses or invent reasons, it can be a good indication to suspect that the young person may be starting to suffer from Internet addiction.

Rule that cannot be applied to girls, since these, despite suffering lower levels of Internet addiction, when they do, it is not expressed with less sincerity within the family, which in turn makes it more difficult the detection and therefore its intervention to overcome it.

This would indicate that children are more sensitive to suffer from this type of addiction related to new technologies, which will have a negative impact on the quality of family life by trying to "hide" their addiction.

All this can be used to establish prevention programs among the students themselves, so that they develop tools with which face Internet addiction, and even among parents, so that they have clear understanding of the first symptoms of addiction to be able to intervene as soon as possible.

Although the results are clear, more research is needed to reach conclusions in this regard, since it is a study focused on a population with specific characteristics, the country not being among the top ten at the level of number of Internet users, employed daily by a little more than half of the current population (53.3%), far behind countries such as Norway, Iceland, Netherlands, Sweden or

Denmark, all of them above 90%, according to data collected by Internet world stats.

It must be taken into account that the consequences of cyberaddiction are considered as an expression of a behavioral addiction, which must be overcome with the intervention of a specialist, and that in many cases requires as a first step to cut off all minor access to the Internet, such and as would be done with other types of addictions.

Cyberbullying:

Another of the dangers of the Internet is cyberbullying, which is an extension of the phenomenon of harassment using technological means on this occasion, either by telephone or by Internet through which a person (stalker) treats to undermine and undermine the self-esteem of another (harassed or bullied), sending threatening, intimidating or blackmail messages through e-mail or instant messaging services (Chat or Messenger type), SMS or social networks.

Before the use of technology was extended, in the phenomenon of bullying, harassment or mistreatment there was a face-to-face encounter between the bully and the bullied, usually accompanied by insults, threats 6-and teasing, and could also lead to physical aggression as a way to achieve what the bully wanted, but what is the incidence of school buying among the population?

This is what is being discovered from the Krishna University Institute of Medical Sciences (India) whose results have been published in the International Journal of Health Sciences and Research.

Four hundred small schoolchildren participated in the study, aged between 8 and 14, of which two hundred were girls.

Each of them was asked with a semi-structured interview based on a standardized questionnaire to detect school bullying called Olweus Bully / Victim Questionnaire, hence two groups were extracted, those who suffered from bullying or had suffered it in the last year and those who don't.

All of them were passed a questionnaire to assess the levels of health and anxiety through the standardized instrument K.I.V.P.A.

The results show a high level of bullying since among the four hundred participants, one hundred thirty-six had suffered in the last year, of which fifty-nine were girls and the rest were boys.

Analyzing the specific type of bullying, it was observed how direct physical aggression was the most common, reaching 60% of cases, followed by insults (37.5%) and rumors (28%).

Among the symptoms experienced by the children were stomach pain (24%), depression (23%), headache (20%), and frequent school absences (18%).

Of all those who suffered from bullying only 24% had informed their parents or teachers about their situation.

Although the study is very localized and cannot be extracted from other populations, it is important to highlight the high numbers of students affected, the different ways of expressing themselves, as well as the low percentage of complaints of those affected.

In recent years, and thanks to awareness campaigns, especially in schools aimed at both teachers and parents, the number of cases of direct harassment has been reduced, giving way to the new phenomenon of cyberbullying, thanks to the misuse of mobile devices and the misuse of the Internet, in addition to the idea of anonymity in the network, which gives the stalker some belief of impunity for his/her actions.

Some experts distinguish between cyber harassment and cyberbullying, the first being the one that occurs through the use of new technologies, restricting the term of cyberbullying only to cases where the harassment comes from the same, peers of similar age or a little older, but who normally share the same place of study, in both cases they share the use of technological devices as a means of bullying.

Of particular concern is the increasing number of cases among adolescents, for example, in Spain almost a third of those under 17 years of age claim to have suffered cyberbullying, and even 19% admit to having insulted through the network. In Latin America, according to S.R.C.A.E. (Second Regional Comparative and Explanatory Study) conducted by the U.N.E.S.C.O. (United Nations Educational, Scientific and Cultural Organization), whose data were obtained between 2005 and 2009, more than 50% of elementary students have been victims of bullying, a danger that is enhanced in the network.

This situation of cyberbullying is going to have the same negative consequences for the harassed, both in psychological and physical health, which has even led some to lose their lives, due to the despair that generates not seeing a way out of this harassment. Hence the importance of raising awareness about this problem in recent years, promoted from different institutions through prevention and education programs, aimed both at young people to inform against, and for parents and teachers to give an appropriate answer to a situation that are new to them. But if the school is becoming the most conducive place for this type of bullying, can cyberbullying be confronted from the school itself?

This is what we tried to find out from the University of Regents and the University of City (England) whose results have been published in the International Journal of Emotional Education.

Twenty university students between the ages of 21 and 30 participated in the study, of which seventeen were women.

They were divided into three groups, the harassed, the bully and the "spectators." Each of them was given a role, which as a role-play they had to interpret and put themselves in the "skin" of their character, commenting among the members of the group the feelings and emotions that generated, for last make a sharing of the different groups

The qualitative results suggest that students identify easily with the role of the stalker, considering the harassed as responsible for their situation, feeling him/her as unsuccessful and marginalized, being difficult to put himself/herself in the role of the harassed.

Which indicates that it is necessary to work on the figure of the stalker and the violence involved, as something "socially acceptable" in a competitive world, you also have to work on the role of the harassed, to be able to correctly convey your image, to show it as a victim and not as a "social loser."

Although the results are revealing as to the feelings on which we have to work, we still have to transform it into an educational intervention program that can be incorporated into other schools and universities, thereby effectively combating this "epidemic" of cyberbullying. That so far does not seem to stop if it is not by denouncing the corresponding institution.

After each complaint there is a whole mechanism behind, in which different public institutions such as the police or the judicial system which try to ensure the safety of Internet users, but can only intervene if they have knowledge of cyberbullying. The importance of parents and teachers being able to detect the initial symptoms of harassment, is essential in order to stop this before it has negative consequences for the physical and mental health of the child.

CHAPTER 3. NETWORK OPPORTUNITES

But technology not only entails dangers for its users, but also offers great opportunities for those who are able to train, adapt and use accordingly. Technology is currently part of the production system, being essential for the proper performance of any activity, but also, when you people leave their job, we can also find leisure activities occupying a good part of their time, almost without realizing it.

The young people who have been called as technological natives, have practically been born with the rise of technology through touchpads, smartphone and using immediate communication systems such as Facebook, Twitter or Tuenti. They see as "normal" and even essential the use of these technologies for any activity they are going to do.

Those who have a few more years, those that technology has come to their life when they were already trained, are called technological migrants, and they have to make real efforts to be able to "keep up" with the advances and new applications or devices , since for them it is still a new tool to which they have to devote a lot of time to be able to master it, but to what extent do we properly use technology to look for jobs?

If we define intelligence as the ability to give a correct response to a demand, technological intelligence would be something like the ability to properly use technology when responding to a demand.

Thus, a person who is not able to use technology conveniently, is not only "lagging behind", but is losing job opportunities or a promotion in his/her job, since the ones who do not respond properly will be replaced by another who can.

Such is the case of competitiveness when looking for a job, although a few years ago, the job seemed guaranteed, the job being transmitted from parents to children, nowadays one must compete with others to get a job.

And as in any other area, technology has also entered into this, so employers no longer place ads in newspapers, but instead hire recruitment companies that advertise applications online, collect resumes, filter and interview a few of them before selecting the ideal candidate for the position.

For which, anyone who wants access to a job must know how to use technology conveniently to be able to first find out about the demand of the job, and then respond appropriately to it.

Something that seems to be implanted in each country at different speeds, this evolution can be observed thanks to the data provided by the European Union's open government on the percentage of the population aged between 16 and 64 who use Internet to look for a job or to send an online curriculum. There is a tendency towards increasing this percentage year after year, which indicates that those who have better management in them would be more likely than those who do not. Being in 2013 the average of users around 17%, amount considerably higher than the scarce 10% of 2004.

The countries of northern Europe: Sweden (29%), Iceland, Norway and Finland (27%) and the United Kingdom (26%), have traditionally been those that have held higher percentages of using the Internet to find work. On the contrary, those who have shown less Internet use in 2013 have been the Czech Republic and Turkey (6%) and Romania (8%).

In the case of Spain, there are only records since 2007 with 10%, progressively increasing this percentage to double in 2013, thus being above the European average.

As you can see, all countries have evolved towards greater use of technology in this area of employment demand through the use of the Internet, which accounts for the progress of this type of communication between employer and candidate.

It remains to be known if these observed trends are

maintained in areas other than labor, being able to determine the "progress" of society based on the level of technological involvement in their most common daily activities.

It is still necessary to verify whether these advances are the same according to gender and age, since gender differences would not be expected, but a higher percentage of technological use would be expected to find work among the youth population compared to those of older age. In spite of which, the results are a clear indication of how it is evolving towards an intensive use of the Internet to find work through the network, since no company currently considers not to use a text processor or e-mail to communicate with your customers, in addition to taking care of your presence on the Internet through a website that is why you should not be surprised if any day you are "quoted" for a job interview via Skype.

Skype is perhaps the best known and most widespread of a series of video-oriented programs, today there are new alternatives that are beginning to be imposed as Google Hangouts, but regardless of the program we use to do it, what are the keys for a job interview through videoconferencing?

From the employer's point of view, that is to say, the person in charge of the selection of personnel in charge of the interview has had to adapt to this new reality, varying the interview with respect to the traditional face-to-face, since now, many of the keys that serve to determine the level of self-confidence, anxiety and even truthfulness of what the interviewee says are not available. The body posture, the way of sitting or crossing the legs, the movement of the hands or feet during the interview have usually been used to get to know the candidate better, but what now? What should we look at?

- The first is in the Nick of the account, which says a lot about the profile he/she uses to communicate on the Internet with others, so whether it is his/her own name or some personal quality will be taken into account as positive. If instead, refers to a hobby it can give an image of lack of formality. That does not mean that you cannot have the Nick you want, but when conducting a job interview it is convenient to use a personal one that gives a good image of oneself.

- In case of technical connection problems, for example, when interrupted and having to reconnect because of internet connections, the way in which the interviewee responds, with peace of mind, patience and above all professionalism will be key in the evaluation.

- The way of dressing, more or less formal by the interviewee, gives an impression of the interest he/she exhibits in achieving the job, so if he/she is in his/her leisure clothe, because in fact he/she is at home, it can be interpreted as "carelessness" "or lack of interest, unlike if he/she goes with a jacket or at least more neatly, just as you would in a face-to-face interview.

- The tone of the conversation, that this does not become a chat between friends, also shows interest in achieving the position.

- Although there may always be unforeseen events, there are some tips that can indicate that this is improvised, showing a lack of interest since the necessary previous tests have not been done checked, for example, a corrected illumination of the room and face of the interviewee, a sound that is too low or that has a lot of interference, that a relative or friend crosses the camera while the interview is on its way, are indicative of "neglect" in the preparation of the same, although as indicated everything must be nuanced, as unforeseen events can always arise.

- On the background that is seen in the back of the interviewee, if it is a blank wall, if we have pictures, photos or a messy bookshelf, all this provides clues as to how they are.

- If it is "bad" to arrive late for the job interview because there was no parking and nowhere to leave the car, what justification can be given if one is not punctual to a Skype interview?

- Of course, the hygiene shown, it is one thing to be at home and another thing is to go to an interview, even by Skype without shaving, without putting "effort", all this shows a lack of interest in the interview.

- Although non-formal language is fundamental in communication, with Skype there is little that can be seen, perhaps the movement of the hands, or of the body in case it occurs, that is why this time the importance of verbal language, both in terms of the background of the discourse and in the form, taking into account aspects of language such as cadence, tone and fluency.

- In addition, the correct use of Skype indicates a certain level of computer management, essential today in most jobs.

Despite all of the above, it should be borne in mind that the Skype interview is nothing more than a tool and is probably an initial step in which to filter certain candidates, just like the initial exam of the curriculum, in the that are discarded for future interviews, to those who do not meet the required profile.

A personal interview or performance observation during the trial period will be decisive in corroborating a correct choice of the best candidate for the job.

As we see in this section, the use of new technologies is changing the way we interact even in the workplace, which is why people who do not know how to adapt will be relegated in favor of those who are managed adequately with the use of the Internet and the new technological tools that have emerged in recent years.

CHAPTER 4. THE AVATAR AND THEIR DIGITAL ID

One of the most remarkable processes of the baby apart from growing, is to see how little by little he/she becomes aware of him/herself, forming a personality that gives him/her a unique identity and different from the rest. In this process of differentiation, the mother will play a prominent role, with whom at first, she will share a symbiosis that causes her not to differentiate herself from him/her. The mother is the one who meets all your needs of care and feeding, but soon that "source of satisfaction" is going to become a "source of frustration", this will happen when the mother does not attend immediately to him/her requirements, for example, of feeding, or that she does not dedicate all the time that the little one demands.

This is the first moment in which a distinction is made between the baby as an individual and the "other", the mother, this experiential knowledge will be consolidated as the child takes control of his/her own body, thus creating the concept of personal image in which more and more elements will be included, from the most obvious, fingers, hands, feet, to others that will be discovered as they are formed and that will have to do with the dominant features of their personality.

The baby will go through different stages until he/she realizes that he/she is "lonely" before the outside world, and that this is composed of others that sometimes heed their requirements and sometimes not. The baby has a great challenge ahead of him/her and is to be trained as a person, independent and differentiated from the "others", which will always have an important role since they will serve as a model to identify, while it helps to compare yourself with others.

The "other" will be present for the rest of our life's, because, thanks to them we are tall and others are short, fat and others are thin, with the "other" we are what we are, more or less than others, wanting what the "other" has achieved or has, becoming a source of personal motivation.

But so far, we are talking about personal identity as a unitary, univocal and stable concept over time, instead we must remember that this identity is composed of different parts such as:

- Body image, where what we think about how we are physically comes in, what we are able or not to do with our muscles (running, swimming) as well as their limits. Recall that this is an important factor in certain psychopathologies in which it is distorted, as is the case with anorexia.

- The mental image of ourselves, that is, the consideration we have about mental abilities and their limits (more or less intelligent), a fundamental aspect on which coaching works, since the limits we believe we have are the first that must be overcome in order to face the difficulties and achieve the objectives we want.

- Sexual identity, which refers to how we feel as a man or as a woman, regardless of the phenotype (differential physical sexual attributes).

- Social identity, which refers to how we feel in different groups of coexistence in which we participate, be it family, school, work, but also groups of colleagues and friends.

Currently, given the importance of technology in all areas of life, a new category has been incorporated:

- Digital identity, which refers to how we look on the web, based on interests, desires and hobbies, but also in the identification with your Nick, profile picture or avatar, establishing new social relationships by belonging to communities, forums or fan groups where you interact.

Society is built with the transmission of ways of thinking, values and norms, but in the digital world, those forms are diluted, since one ceases to belong to one place and goes to what is called "Global Village." In this digital world, people can be whatever they want, and introduce themselves to others as they prefer because they have the opportunity to form a new digital identity.

In person, face to face, and without saying anything, you are offering a lot of yourself, how tall you are, what weight, what is the color of hair or skin, even how you dress. All this information is foreign in Internet, and is replaced by what is decided on the digital identity.

Now the behavior does not have to be the same in real life and on the Internet. A person can live humbly at home, and instead of "rubbing shoulders" with bankers or politicians, since the rules by which the network is governed is different.

There is even talk that the network has its own culture, that said, there are ways of thinking, values and norms exclusive to the network, which can hardly exist in real life, and it is not just about having friends spread all over the world , but it is expressed in phenomena as curiosity that of selflessly sharing, whether ones time, files or knowledge.

Thus, in recent years, phenomena such as crowdfunding or collective financing have arisen, whereby a person presents a specific project on a specialized crowdfunding platform to receive financial support from hundreds and even thousands of people, with whom he/she had not previously had contact.

Another phenomenon is Crowd learning, where people share their knowledge unselfishly with the rest, so that a doctor, engineer or mechanic can expose and share their experience and skills, so that others can learn from it.

Some studies have indicated that we are facing a new way of thought, feelings and expressions that an individual expresses, that said, before an authentic e-personality, or virtual personality, an alternative of the individual that uses only on the Internet, but that can even affect to the off-line personality or "real" personality.

The fact that sometimes these personalities do not coincide, is because they are used in different "worlds", where social relationships are established with different people, away from "real" partners and friends.

Years ago the concept of hyper personal communication emerged, to refer to the possibilities offered by the network to be a "better communicator", overcoming the limitations of "reality", without "interference" of how we are physically, expressing ourselves in a way more open and close to the people we meet in a network, thus forming new relationships that otherwise could not be had in real life.

Social networks are currently part of who we are, especially the youngest, influencing the level of narcissism.

The way of expressing oneself in the networks to achieve a greater "virtual" social recognition reinforces the narcissistic behaviors in a network.

If at first some social networks sought to connect friends and classmates, as was the purpose of Facebook, soon friends of "reality" gave way to virtual friends.

It is no longer necessary for you to meet someone to add them to your social networks as a "friend", since the greater the number of people added, the greater your "cache" on the Internet, situations that have even led companies to offer a great number of "friends", hundreds or thousands, for a few dollars.

All this only encourages and reinforces the narcissism of the person, to be "popular", in a virtual world, attention that does not get in his/her "real" life, which encourages this behavior in networks, to increase that pleasant feeling granted by narcissism.

Thus, some authors have pointed out that precisely this narcissism is the real reason why social networks are so successful among the youngest, which are in an evolutionary stage where peers become their source of comparison, the actions being " good or bad "depending on whether" others "approve it or not, but do you know what your level of narcissism is expressed in a network?

This is precisely what is being explored from the National Central University (Taiwan) whose results have been published in the scientific journal "Psychology".

Four hundred seventy-one university students aged 19

to 24 years participated in the study, of which two hundred and twenty-one were women.

All of them responded to N.P.I.-40 (Narcissistic Personality Inventory), with the aim of validating the forty items that made it up and the narcissism factors that were evaluated, specifically seven, the degree of influence of the person on a network; the degree of influence of others when making decisions on a network; the degree to which people feel "bright" and superior in a network; the degree of exposing everything in the network; the tendency to manipulate others in a network; the degree to which one looks for oneself in a network; and the degree to which you believe a network provides you with benefits in your life.

The results show the validity and reliability of the test developed, correctly assessing the level of narcissism of Internet users.

As the authors have pointed out in their article, not having a tool to assess the level of narcissism on the Internet, was a great obstacle when conducting research with respect to personality on the network.

The creation of an evaluation instrument is always a step forward in knowledge because it allows us to better understand the observed phenomena, so that the number of hours used or the most used social networks can now be compared with the level of narcissism of the user to see if there is a correlation between the two.

Likewise, comparisons can be made with other personality characteristics that are known to have an important influence on social networks, such as the level of obsession of users, which has been seen to positively correlate with their intensive use, being a good source when evaluating possible addictive behaviors within social networks.

When you enter the world of the Internet, we do not do it face to face with people but we use a Nick, or username and an avatar.

The avatar is the character that is used to interact with others on the network, which, in the case of virtual worlds, is usually in three dimensions.

Keeping in some cases a certain resemblance to one's self, and in others it is totally opposite or nothing to do with their physical form. Similarly, when interacting through these avatars, the person can express himself/herself as he/she is, or behave in a way that he/she wouldn't do in "real" life.

Thus, social relationships are established, and can even find themselves a partner, with the avatars of other people whom they may never see in their lives. In spite of which, you can exchange information, experiences and feelings, and even immerse yourself in a subject of interest, all thanks to an online socialization process, based on virtual interactivity where new users are known with whom they share and from which they learn.

My personal experience regarding avatars and virtual worlds is limited, therefore, although I explored the possibility of incorporating some type of therapy through these channels, I soon discovered that they are rather leisure-oriented. Specifically, I explored what is considered the largest community in this area Second Life, with more than one million users and in which hundreds of them are incorporated every day.

Actually, Second Life is an almost infinite succession of virtual worlds, some private, others public, and in each of them, there are microworlds of people who connect and interact more or less regularly.

The free distribution software allows you to have an avatar, a three-dimensional character with which to interact with others, being able to choose any physical quality, such as height, weight, gender or skin color, you can also change your clothes as many times you want, and even go in disguise.

The payment part of Second Life allows you to select many more personal characteristics, clothes, and even rent virtual "lands" where you can build your own microworld, which you can enable as public or private, allowing yourself to invite the people you want.

There are many public places that are "copy" of some famous monument, city or street, so the avatar can move to meet new places, visit museums, or talk to people who are meeting on the street.

One of the aspects that the experts I consulted told me about, when I start to explore this virtual worlds, was that the people with whom I contacted, will hardly provide any information about their "real" life, so regardless of gender, height or weight of the avatar, you will not be able to be sure who is behind it.

Despite these limitations, companies and even educational institutions have seen their potential and have their presence there to bring offers to the users, as well as to provide spaces for them to exchange. A notorious case regarding the dissemination of health-related matters in Second Life, is "Isla de Salud", directed by the S.S.F.C.M. And C. (Spanish Society of Family and Community Medicine) and the Coalition of Citizens with Chronic Diseases, where health professionals meet to give talks and answer the questions posed by users connected at that time.

A large flow of research on digital identity is currently

being developed, trying to understand how it affects everyday life, facilitating or interfering with it, with research to learn how virtual "experienced" feelings affect "real" life.

One of the great advantages of new technologies is that they allow greater democratization, all having the same value when it comes to opinion. At least that was the theory, until opinion leaders began to emerge, who sometimes corresponded to professionals such as journalists or politicians. Bloggers also began to emerge that by their charisma or their way of expressing themselves. Thousands of followers who read them regularly gave great value to their words, so much so that companies give them a chance to advertise their products. Thus, establishing a clear differentiation between users, but if there are differences between Internet users, is there also the possibility of social exclusion through the Internet?

That is precisely what a study by the University of Vienna (Austria) has tried to answer, the results of which have been published in the scientific journal Proceedings of the International Society for Presence Research.

The study involved forty women between the ages of 18 and 29, who developed a series of activities in a virtual world through an avatar while observing their behavior while physiological records were made to compare them.

The experiment also included similar characteristics for another part of the group, but this time they interacted physically, face to face in the same situations.

Half of the group were made to go through a task where an "accomplice" of the experimenter made the participant feel included in what he/she was doing; on the other hand, what the "accomplice" did was to exclude the participant.

The results report that no differences were found in the measures of satisfaction and arousal (the degree of impact of the perceived emotions) evaluated for the participants, which implies that the "virtual experience" of inclusion or exclusion is as "vivid" as face to face reality.

Although the results seem clear, it remains to be asked what would have happened if a group of boys had also been included in the study to compare, probably the effects found even going in the same direction would be more forceful, since aggressiveness shown by men to frustration, or as in this case to the behaviors of exclusion of others, is usually more direct and explosive.

Although the authors do not come to assess the implications of their results, it is clear that, if the line between the virtual and the real does not exist, we must begin to consider what teenagers see or play on the computer, and how they maintain their virtual relationships , a concern that parents have to have, just as they would if their child goes out with friends they don't know or to do something they don't know what it is.

Knowing that the best prevention is education, but in order to educate proper use of the products and services offered on the network, it is important that parents know how to handle themselves properly in order to teach their child how to choose and behave in the virtual world just as they would in person.

CHAPTER 5. THE PSYCHOLOGY ON SOCIAL NETWORKS

Social networks have become the most common form of communication among young people, where they can share and comment on what they think or feel.

This option is growing day by day, and new social networks are created that try to bring new users together.

The advantage of these networks compared to other media such as blogs or forums, is the immediacy of communication.

My experience in social networks is relatively recent, just 2 years old and all following a job interview, in which I was offered to be the director of a Psychology department, but the person who interviewed me thought strange of me by my null presence on the Internet.

At that time my interest in social networks was null, since I kept my contacts through e-mails or on my phone. Although in the end I did not pass the interview, it made me think and reflect that I was missing something, my presence on the Internet, and that it could have negatively influenced the assessment of my curriculum.

So, within a few days I created profiles on Twitter, Facebook and Google+, where I maintain an intense activity, which has been "rewarded" by a multitude of contacts and followers.

In addition, and as part of my commitment to scientific dissemination, I have a blog called Novelties in Psychology, where every article I publish in my blog about the latest advances in the different areas of psychology and neurosciences. Then I share them through my social networks, getting thousands of followers that translate into an average of one thousand visits a day on the blog.

But perhaps the work that I personally feel most proud of is that one achieved on LinkedIn, which unlike the previous ones is a professional network, where I have more than three thousand five hundred mental health professionals who follow me to know the latest publications I do.

Social networks where we dedicate time and energy to respond, share and like, to keep up to date on the latest publications on topics of interest or simply to be in touch with the people we are interested in.

All this is a human activity, which can and should be analyzed, to help us understand and describe what happens in cyberspace, better said, on the Internet.

Currently, a large amount of data is being developed that can be analyzed on the frequency of use, in which networks we spend more time, what we do in each network, with whom we contact, something that in principle does not seem to be of interest, it has been observed that it serves to understand what kind of person we are.

The latest research indicates that, just as everyone is in reality, this is how they will behave on the Internet, so that the study can be done backwards, knowing how they behave on a network we can find out how each one is.

An essential tool for social sciences, such as sociology or social psychology, since it allows us to observe how groups change on the Internet, their interaction, and with it the society where they are.

But it is also of interest at the psychological level, both when detecting psychopathologies and to be able to offer personalized solutions to the user.

Below, the latest psychological research on the Internet is set out according to the social network under study and analysis.

Facebook

Every day we spend more time being connected through the different social networks, either by keeping up to date, or to simply share with others.

If something has characterized this last decade it has been in the inclusion of life of all kinds of social networks aimed at facilitating life. You can talk to a best friend or a colleague on the other side of the world at the stroke of a mouse, while receiving the latest news about what is happening in Japan.

Few things are those that currently cannot be done through social networks, whether they are connected to a chat, a forum, or a discussion group on the topic of interest, where anyone can share and comment on that topic.

Something that has been seen as a danger among minors, since they are who spend more time on social networks, can sometimes have a negative impact on the student's academic performance. But are social networks a reflection of who we are?

This is precisely what Monash University (Malaysia) is investigating, whose results have been published in the scientific journal Cyberpsychology: Journal of Psychosocial Research on Cyberspace.

One hundred fifty-eight university students participated in the study, aged between eighteen and twenty-four, of which 77% were women. Of all the social networks used by these young people, it was decided to choose the social network Facebook, due to the extension and popularity in its use. Para This evaluated the level of intrusion of this social network in daily life through a standardized questionnaire called F.I.Q. (Facebook Intrusion Questionnaire).

Likewise, to observe if this "reflection" of a person

occurs in the network, a personality characteristic was analyzed, such as the level of obsession. For this, participants were evaluated through two standardized questionnaires, the O.C.I.-R. (Obsessive Compulsive Inventory-Revised) and O.B.Q.-20 (Obsessive Belief Questionnaire-20). The investigation tries to discover if their way of behaving Facebook will vary or not depending on the level of obsession of each person.

The results show that obsessive beliefs and behaviors will be significantly reflected in the use of Facebook. So, those students who had higher levels of obsession were also those who made more intensive use of this social network.

Despite the clarity in the results, the limitations of the study must be taken into account, since it is a very specific population with a specific idiosyncrasy such as that of Malaysia, and in addition all participants were university students, so it would require new research before being able to extrapolate the results to all young people.

Another of the limitations of this study is that the information obtained comes from the use of standardized questionnaires, based on the participant's response, and not so much on what he/she really does. Today there are Apps, which are small programs that are installed on a smartphone and that it registers the use made through it, which allows to know exactly how much time is spent on being connected to social networks through their mobile device, which would provide a more reliable measure than the exclusive use of standardized questionnaires.

With these results, it seems clear that in the end it is expressed as each one is in what is done, either by communicating in person, face to face, or through social networks. Thus, and despite the advancement of technology we can still see people talking on the phone shaking hands to give greater impetus to the message they express, even knowing that the other person will not be able to see.

But the previous results lead to consider the following, if it is the same in the real world as in the virtual one, what happens to the roles that each one has to live? Does the network become a place of "liberation " or not?

This is precisely what is being explored jointly from the University of New South Wales (Australia) and the University of Western England (England) whose results have been published in the scientific journal Psychology of Women Quarterly.

The study involved one hundred and fifty university students between the ages of 17 and 25, all of them women, and with a normal average weight, assessed using the weight formula divided by the squared height.

The participants were asked through an online ad-hoc

questionnaire about their habits in the consumption of leisure, television, magazines, music, including social networks, for which they had to identify the number of hours dedicated to each of these activities. In the case of Facebook, they must indicate how often it was reviewed. And in the case of the magazines read they had to tell if these used to be fashionable or not.

Likewise, the tendency of each of them to be compared with the rest was evaluated through the standardized scale called Upward and Downward Appearance Comparison Scale; The same information was requested, but this time about the comparison within the Facebook network, with "friends" and users of that network. Finally, it was evaluated by S.O.Q. (Self-Objectification Questionnaire) the personal image that she had of herself, as an "object" or not.

The results show that the young university students show a high correlation between the use made of Facebook of objectifying women as an object of desire, that is, the social canons of "woman-object" continue to be maintained in the network than that in the real life, since the same results were obtained as in the relationship between women as objects of desire and fashion magazines.

This is the pressure of society that young women especially suffer from having a "pretty face" and a "perfect body", they will suffer both in their real and virtual lives, and that said, all participants had a normal weight, but what would happen to those who are overweight?

If the same pressure is maintained or even less in the network, it is instead becoming a place of leisure and amusement, it can become a continuation of the social norms where it is seen, thus perpetuating the canons of beauty and pressure that young women feel like they are objectified.

One of the main limitations of this study is that the information was extracted through self-reports, when there are currently "tracking" programs capable of identifying what time they are connected, what social media service is used and even who is connected, all information more thorough than the previous one.

It must be taken into account that the population under study have been young university students, so it is necessary to investigate in other populations before being able to establish generalizations in this regard.

In spite of the above, the results seem clear, in that the "social canons" are transmitted and maintained on the network, thereby limiting the possibilities offered by the Internet when creating and maintaining a digital identity, independent of the "social demands" of the place where one lives.

Something that is worrisome, since it means that in the "macho societies", the values that are instilled and imposed, will continue to remain among young woman, even if they are in a virtual world.

As the authors of the study suggest, it is a first approach to this problem of digital image among young people, being necessary the incorporation of new research that is able to better explain this phenomenon, and also serves to establish prevention plans , so that the image of women as an object of desire does not continue to spread.

Since social networks have broken into the lives of young people, there has been a new phenomenon, that of Internet addiction.

Although the phenomenon of cyberaddiction is recent, it has evolved rapidly, so the first persons to be addicted to video games or the Internet spent hours and hours without leaving their rooms, unable to disconnect from role-playing games or any other video game to add more points and increase in world rankings; as if that was the most important thing in the world.

From these first cases, the term "Hikikomori" syndrome emerged, originally identified in Japan during the 1980s and 1990s. Young people who suffered from it literally turned their backs on society, and refused to interact with others, if not through computers.

Something that sometimes led to poor nutrition and even abandonment of personal hygiene.

Examples of this have been observed to a greater or lesser extent along the globe, where the computer screen becomes the "reality" of the young man, there being nothing beyond the four walls of their rooms.

Currently, and thanks to mobile devices, such as touchpads, iPads or smartphones, it is no longer necessary to stay home to be connected to the Internet.

In addition, a few years ago the incursion of social networks has made communication possibilities increase beyond video games or chats, which has resulted in an increase in the number of cases of Internet addiction, but what is the percentage of Facebook addicts?

This is precisely what has been attempted from the Department of Systems Information and the Department of Fundamentals of Education and Social Sciences, Faculty of Education, Technological University of Malaysia (Malaysia), together with the Department of Computing and Technology of Information, Azad Islamic University (Iran) whose results have just been published in the scientific International Journal of Information and Education Technology.

Four hundred forty-one university students with an average of 24 years participated in the study, of which 49% were women.

All were evaluated using the standardized scale to know the level of addiction to Facebook called B.F.A.S. (Bergen Facebook Addiction Scale), the level of locus of control was also evaluated through the L.O.C. (Locus of Control) and the level of personal selfishness through Barron's Ego Strength Scale; In addition, information about the religion and origin of the student was collected.

The results inform that young people showed very high levels of addiction to Facebook, reaching 47% of them, this means that almost half of Facebook users were addicted to this social network.

These results are maintained despite the origin (Malay or non-Malaysian), religion they practiced (Muslim, Christian, Buddhist, etc.) and even gender of the participants.

The authors do not evaluate these data or the implications on the mental health of young people, nor on their social relationships.

One of the limitations of the study is that the selection of the participants was made among those who regularly used social networks, that said, the results reflect that these high levels of addiction occur among regular users, but says nothing about those young people who don't use social networks so often.

It must be taken into account that the study was carried out only with university students, not being able to extend the results to the rest of the population, not even to the youth, since they may be influencing such outstanding variables as the socio-economic level or the culture of Facebook users, aspects that are not analyzed in this study.

Although the authors of the study have opted to analyze Facebook levels, due to the popularity of this network, and its increasing number of users, which has currently been counted in about two billion; A comparative analysis with other social networks has not been carried out to try to understand if it is a phenomenon of Facebook, or any other network such as twitter or google +.

So, it requires new replicas to establish in this regard.

It will also be necessary to take into account if Facebook addicts are addicted exclusively to this social network, or to others or all; what I would be talking about more than a "problem" with Facebook, a problem of the individual's personality that is reflected in his/her use of the Internet.

But to know the answer to this question, the design must be improved, incorporating questions about the use of other social networks and their frequency of use.

Twitter

One of the main problems of a professional, caregiver or family member of an affected patient with autism spectrum disorder is being properly informed. Although we can all have some general ideas about autism, until a family member does not present a problem with this disorder, there is no need to deepen the knowledge about its origin, triggers, evolution and especially treatment.

Until a few years ago, access to this specialized information was difficult even for professionals who had to do refresher courses to be able to know the progress that was being made in this regard. The consultations to the libraries have given way to the yearbooks of the magazines, and from there to the specialized portals, to the web pages of foundations, federations and associations.

Nowadays, with the development and popularization of the Internet, being up to date on the subject of your interest has become a relatively easier task for any professional, caregiver or family member of a patient with autism spectrum disorder, despite which social network is necessary to go to be up to date, be it Facebook, Google+ or Twitter. But can Twitter help Autism Spectrum Disorder?

At least this is what they believe from the Pattern Recognition and Data Analysis Center of the Deakin University and the National ICT (Australia) who presented their results in the 2014 IEEE / ACM International Conference on Advances in Social Network Analysis and Mining.

In this case there are no participants, since it is a mathematical analysis of the Tweets that have been sent over the Internet with the English words of "autism", "add", "autism awareness", "Asperger" and "aspie" In total, 944,568 Tweets issued between August 26, 2013 and November 25 of the same year were analyzed.

The main result is about the validity of the information with high value, issued by public administrations, which is shared through Twitter on the theme of Autism Spectrum Disorder, with this information prevailing, compared to what can be generated by Any particular user.

As the authors of the study indicate is the first time this type of research is carried out, which opens the doors to the study and analysis of the different psychopathologies through social networks, to understand how the interests of institutions, relatives and caregivers of patients affected by one or another psychopathology are evolving.

This has the disadvantage that the data is only descriptive, but it cannot be compared with any previous result, which allows us to understand the evolution of the use of these concepts. Despite the limited results, what the study shows is the importance that social networks are increasingly having both for professionals, caregivers and family members of patients with Autism Spectrum Disorder, not only to keep up of the latest developments in research stories, but even to share feelings of support among users, which reinforces the work done from the family associations of patients.

Personally, I did not know all this thematic of the analysis of large sums of data coming from the Internet, called Big Data, so I have entered this subject, and I have realized that it is an area still unexplored for psychology. An analysis of thousands or millions of data in which to look for patterns with which to understand and predict human behavior.

In the company vibe it is used to know how its customers and users behave, to later try to predict the behavior through statistical analyzes and thereby optimize the benefits of the companies. My case is that I am interested in the subject of mental health and I try to tie it up with "Big Data".

To know what is being talked about on the Internet about this topic, there are several options, the easiest way is to assess the number of groups or forums, but with that given information I would only know where the interest of each individual resides in each of the specific topics of mental health.

But to know what is happening on the network, it is best to do it through some of the most used direct communication tools such as microblogging's and Twitter, so I started my first study with "Big Data" to answer, how much do you talk on Twitter about mental health?

The analysis was carried out on Twitter traffic regarding mental health issue, all analyzed thanks to the collaboration of the CartoDB company. To delimit the concept of mental health, four of the most prominent terms were chosen, two corresponding to adulthood, related to neurodegenerative diseases, and two to childhood, on developmental disorders: Parkinson's Disease, Alzheimer's Disease, Attention Deficit Hyperactivity Disorder, and Autism Spectrum Disorder, respectively. What leaves out other equally important topics such as those of Mood Disorders, especially Major Depression Disorder; or Addiction Disorders or those of Eating Behavior.

For this study, all Tweets published during a full day of the previous week were analyzed. In total, 11,500 geolocated Tweets distributed around the world have been analyzed, using the statistical package SPSS v. 22, of which, the first thing to indicate is that there is a different distribution depending on the theme of the conversation. Thus, the subjects related to mental health in adults were

56% (three thousand five hundred Tweets on Alzheimer's Disease and three thousand Tweets on Parkinson's Disease); being 44% relative to the subject in childhood (two thousand five hundred Tweets on Attention Deficit Hyperactivity Disorder and two thousand five hundred on Autism Spectrum Disorder).

Keep in mind that the search terms on Twitter have been in English, using the keywords: "Parkinson"; "Alzheimer", "ADHD" and "Autism", which means that the results have to be taken with care especially in regard to countries that do not speak English, in fact, 8,171 Tweets were written in English (71, 05%); compared to 1,252 in Spanish (10.88%), which makes between the two, 82% of the total, plus another thirty-two more languages throughout the world.

Regarding the distribution of Tweets in each of the four search terms according to language, report that 57% of Tweets in English are on the subject of children's mental health and 43% of Tweets to health Mental in adults.

In the case of the Spanish language, 99% of Tweets corresponded to mental health in adults, since the search terms are used the same in Spanish as in English. On the other hand, the respective terms of children's mental health are different, hence their low percentage. Review that, within mental health in adults, 72% corresponds to the theme of Alzheimer's, while 37% corresponds to the theme of Parkinson's.

As was the case in the previously mentioned study, as it is an innovative form of research, there are still not enough studies with which to make a comparison, so new research is required before conclusions can be obtained.

Regarding the way in which we use Twitter, below, I transcribe the interview I conducted on this subject to Dr. David Lavilla Muñoz, Professor of Digital Communication and New Trends of the European University:

- What is #informetwitter and what is its objective?

The #informetwitter is an investigation, registered with the OTRI, carried out from the European University of Madrid together with two expert companies in Internet and Social Networks to know how the user of this microblog behaves.

Thus, the EMU, the Redbility company and Influenzia company have drawn conclusions about what is the most efficient way to communicate and participate in this social network from three qualitative methodologies: Eye Tracking, Emotional evaluation, morphological and syntactic analysis of the message.

- How did #informetwitter arise?

It arises from an initial idea of the Redbility company

to get to know the user of this social network better and help companies manage Twitter and communicate better through this platform.

- How many people collaborated on #informetwitter?

More than fifty people collaborated in this investigation. These includes advanced Twitter users, Redbility professionals, Influencers and those of the European University of Madrid.

- How did they work on #informetwitter?

The Redbility company was in charge of the technological tools necessary to carry out the study, in order to propose its subsequent analysis of the same data extraction. Influezia, contributed the knowledge of the expert users in the use and management of the social network and the Master of Digital Journalism and Social Networks of the European University of Madrid gave the seal of university quality, its certification and the commitment to generate academic analysis from of the data obtained.

- What is the population under study by #informetwitter?

Redbility used different qualitative techniques to

analyze the sample consisting of thirty-five participants divided into expert users (heavy users) and medium users (medium users), - and thus analyze their information. Among the techniques were direct observation, emotional analysis, morphosyntactic analysis and eye tracking and the study subject was divided according to its device of use. All these users were extracted from the database managed by Influenza, a leading company in Spain, as expert users, with media coverage on the Internet, of a universe of one hundred and thirty users with the characteristics requested to carry out the study.

- What are the results achieved by #informetwitter?

The conclusions, more exhaustively, can be observed at this   address: http://www.redbility.com/downloads/Conclusiones_sobre_l a_investigacion_del_comportamiento_de_los_usuarios_en_ Twitter.pdf. However, among the most significant stand out:

a. That Twitter feeds personal ego.

b. That the wait in the opening of links generates anxiety.

c. That a tweet with abbreviations and unstructured does not work.

d. That if humor and irony are used, the tweet will be

more successful

e. That writing well communicates better

f. That the tweets sent first thing in the morning are the most read.

- What are the objectives to be achieved in the future by #informetwitter?

The #informetwitter group now presents a doctoral thesis that deals with the online reputation made by the professor of the European University of Madrid Mercedes Agüero Pérez. This is to verify that all this virtual boom in business communication does not cease to entail risks since the Internet user himself/herself can enter into conversations with other users or companies horizontally, without hierarchies and thus benefiting or damaging his/her reputation. In this thesis, in addition, we have tried to make a series of recommendations to companies to try to favor the management of their reputation based on common parameters observed in the advanced users of this social network.

CHAPTER 6. PSYCHO TECHNOLOGY

But technology is not only used to contact, share or comment, it can also be used to bring therapy to each person's home, without having to move around, it is called online or virtual psychotherapy.

This is an option that is increasingly having more followers, especially in younger audiences, because it allows them to reconcile their day-to-day, while receiving psychological therapy without leaving their home.

Despite the reluctance of some health professionals, and the limitations on the observation of the nonverbal behavior of the patient by the specialist, the advantages are unquestionable.

According to my experience in recent years, the patient feels much less self-conscious when talking and sharing, it is true that nonverbal behavior can be diminished, but the incorporation of the webcam with video calls partially replaces that difficulty, the results being the same as those that can be achieved in face-to-face consultation.

But if so far we have seen how technological media have different incidence among its users, there is still a field to comment, and that is when that technology is used for the design and implementation of specific software for the treatment of some psychopathology, to accompany and help to the training of certain skills and abilities.

There are multiple technological applications designed for the field of psychology, from those that try to bring therapy home, through online psychotherapy, to software created to help the treatment of patients or training some cognitive skills as memory.

One of the greatest cognitive incidents on life is when working memory is affected, since this causes great problems when it comes to work, damaging its autonomy. Working memory is one that allows working in the here and now, remembering what has to be done, to follow an objective or task.

If the working memory is injured, the person may find himself totally "lost", since he/she starts an activity, such as going to buy the bread, and halfway there their memory goes "blank" and now they don't where they were going or why. Likewise, when a dialogue is held with another person, that type of memory is required, to follow "the thread" of the conversation. If this ability is damaged, the person will soon be "lost" and will not know what they are talking about or will tend to repeat the same arguments over and over again, because they do not remember saying them before.

The affectation of working memory occurs both from the normal aging of the person and from some psychopathologies such as Alzheimer's disease, but cases can also be seen in young people affected with A.D.H.D. (Attention Deficit Hyperactivity Disorder), where some authors argue that by improving working memory, children with A.D.H.D. significantly improve their ability to concentrate and sustain their attention, being able to maintain similar levels to the rest of their peers.

As we can see, it is important to know what working memory consists of, but, above all, to know if you can train satisfactorily when it has been observed that it starts to fail.

That is precisely what has been tried to find out with a study conducted jointly by the University of Oregon, the Louisiana University of Technology, the University of California, and the Rose-Hulman Institute of Technology (USA) whose results have been published in the scientific journal, "Journal of Behavioral and Brain Science".

The study involved thirty young people aged 18 to 31 years, who were assigned to one of the following three experiments: Initial evaluation; Training experiment; Transfer Evaluation. All these experiments were performed by putting the subject in front of the computer screen while being asked to perform a task that involved their working memory.

Only half of the subjects who were trained for two

hours a day for twelve weeks participated in the training phase. At the end all participants, with and without training, went through transfer evaluation to see if there were differences between them.

The results report that there were no differences between the two groups in the first experiment, while in the transfer evaluation phase they showed significant improvements in the group that received specific training on working memory.

In addition to the behavioral measures discussed above, the research collected the electrical activity of the brain showing how trained participants had greater activity in the prefrontal areas of the brain, precisely where it has been observed that working memory is involved.

Although the study has been conducted with few participants, it seems to positively indicate about the expected benefits by significantly improving their working memory in just twenty-four hours of training.

Based on the above, it is still necessary to adapt the experimental materials for their use in the different populations to which it is intended to be applied in order to guarantee its effectiveness in both young and old. Since it is a breakthrough, knowing that with "small" training you can recover a cognitive capacity as important and fundamental in everyday life as working memory.

This would be an example of how the scientific design of training software for certain cognitive skills offers guarantees as to the expected results.

For some years now, the misconception that Alzheimer's can be prevented by just practicing twenty minutes a day with Brain-training programs is being generalized. Among the advocates of this opinion are, of course, the designers and creators of these training programs.

Apps and software for smartphones that are sold as the mental health panacea are not lacking. Defending that, just as one goes to a gym to keep fit with regular and periodic exercises, their mind equally exercised for fifteen or twenty minutes a day with one of their programs will keep the mind in shape.

In fact, they base this theory on some studies that validate the effectiveness of doing something versus doing nothing. Thus, a multitude of computer programs have been developed for memory, attention, perfection or any other cognitive capacity that can be trained. In some cases, it involves incorporating traditional neuropsychological training sessions into the computer. The most current programs are sold adapted to the level of the performance of each person, but are mental training programs useful for the fight against Alzheimer's?

From the professional associations of psychology and the research centers of the United States, the effectiveness of these programs has been questioned. Pointing out that the lack of scientific rigor in its design and the fact that not having a professional to supervise them prevents checking the effectiveness in patients. In addition, they warn of the subsequent dangers of abandoning other healthy practices, focusing exclusively on the supposed benefits of these programs, just as would happen if someone tries to go on a diet through the intake of pills, without doing anything to control the quantity and quality of what they eat or without even doing daily exercises.

Knowing that in the case of neurodegenerative diseases such as Alzheimer's disease, where there is a biological basis of deterioration at the neuronal level, the effectiveness of these programs has not been proven, giving patients and family members false hopes about a product that is not initially designed to fight Alzheimer's disease.

That is why we must know to what extent it is a "mental game", which serves to entertain and maintain some cognitive skills, but with a rather limited effectiveness. Going for a walk, reading books or having a good conversation with a family member or friend, have a higher incidence on the brain than mental training games.

Therefore, these new developments must be put to their fair value, knowing that when the disease occurs, the specialist's instructions should be followed exclusively and not try to find "shortcuts" or use tools that are not sufficiently validated.

Following is the interview with Dr. Daniela Galindo Bermúdez, President of Talking with Julis: the solution for communication and learning for people with disabilities.

- What is "Talking with Julis" and what is the goal?

Talking to Julis, it is a non-profit institution that creates communication and learning solutions for people with disabilities.

The basis of the development of any person is in the communication, if their needs, feelings or thoughts cannot be expressed, it will not be understood before the outside world by limiting us access to educational, work and social spaces.

"Talking to Julis" is that solution so that anyone can communicate their wishes to another person without the problems of understanding one another. All through images, voices, words and sign language videos.

Communicating is not just talking, it is also reading and writing; Many of our users have difficulties in speaking, reading and / or writing, but thanks to "Talking with Julis" they have found that the tools that reinforces these needs are based on their abilities.

- How did "Talking to Julis" arise and who is it for?

"Talking with Julis" was born of a personal challenge. My sister Julis, has a disability to speak. She listens perfectly but does not speak. From a very young age, she learned to communicate through sign language, but: What if she wanted to say something to her grandmother? Or what if she wanted to buy something? NOBODY WOULD TO UNDERSTAND BECAUSE NOBODY WOULD LEARN SIGN LANGUAGE FOR HER.

My dad a little restless before this difficulty, decided to make a tool that would allow her to communicate with anyone and that anyone could also communicate with her and that is the result of "Talking to Julis".

Today our solution is being used by people with Down Syndrome, Autism, Cerebral Palsy, Cognitive Deficit, Deaf, Deaf-Blind, and people who due to illness or accident lost the ability to speak.

- Is any minimum capacity required to use Talking with Julis?

Talking to Julis does not require any minimum capacity to use it. Depending on each case, the solution is adapted so that you can use it. For example:

a. People with motor difficulties do not have the possibility of using a computer. Each person is different, so we would analyze the best way they would approach the team. There are external aids such as hardware that facilitates the use of the computer such as big mouse, licorne, pointers, among others. If this does not work, we have worked with the help of someone else where the personal user indicates (no matter the form) the image you want to select and the assistant person goes and chooses it for him.

b. People who find it difficult to synchronize the use of their mouse: Today there are several "touch" computers that eliminate the use of the mouse. If there is no possibility of obtaining one, there is the option of having external help to assist you in choosing the vocabulary to communicate. Within our experience, people we have encountered that cannot handle a mouse, with activities of interest in relation to their communication and their activities; We have achieved that a patient would handle the equipment with total autonomy.

For "Talking to Julis" disability is not a limitation, it is just a different way of doing things. There are always a thousand ways to do what is proposed, we just need a little more dedication and commitment to achieve the proposed goals.

- What does "Talking to Julis" contribute to other software oriented to neurolinguistic rehabilitation?

"Talking to Julis" allows the understanding (decoding) of language more clearly and closer to the person, through the relationship between the image, the word and the voice; Having the possibility to observe, remember and relate these three pillars through the use of "Talking with Julis".

At the level of the expression, the person has the possibility of finding more easily the images-words he needs to communicate. We all think what we want to communicate through images that when pronounced become words. Talking to Julis, for those who present difficulties in their oral communication, it becomes an easy, practical and effective method that allows a mental image to be externalized in a software image, also allowing a better understanding of what the interlocutor wishes to express.

In the case of learning to read and write, in addition to the advantage of having images, words, voices and signs (for their users); the visualization of the colored frames that accompany the different groups of words, give the person a better understanding of the grammatical structure, allowing him to write and being aware of the proper use of the grammar elements and the intention of a text (if it is a question, an affirmation, an admiration, among others) and read keeping in mind the organization of the words and therefore the understanding of the message.

- Under what operating systems does it work, Windows, Mac, Linux? Under what circumstances does it work on PC, Touchpads, Smartphone?

Talking to Julis works for Windows Operating Systems and is downloadable on computers.

- What are the achievements of Talking with Julis?

"Talking to Julis" has reached more than four thousand two hundred people in Latin America who today benefit from a different and efficient communication. They are people who are being included in their families, in their education, labor and social institutions.

On the other hand, "Talking to Julis" has had great National and International awards.:

In 2013 we obtained second place in an award organized by Cisco Systems at the International Level. The "Connecting the Unconnected" award gave us first place as the best Story and Second place at the general level.

Also, in 2013, we obtained an Honorable Mention from the Colombian Ministry of Culture in the C3 + d Laboratory.

In 2014, we were named as finalists of the Entrepreneurship World Cup: Mass Challenge, which is organized in Boston, United States; and who bring together the one hundred and twenty-eight companies in the world with the greatest potential for growth, impact and innovation.

- What are the objectives to be achieved in the future by Talking to Julis?

Our objectives:

* Reach all the people who need Talking with Julis to find that communicative and learning solution.

* Create a social impact where people do not view disability as something limiting but as a different way of doing things that lead to results where they have the same educational, work and social opportunities.

* Change the perception of disability through visible and viable results for real social inclusion.

This is only possible thanks to the support of people and companies that decide to support Talking with Julis on their way to deliver the complete solution to all people.

But the specific applications do not only remain there, but currently experimental studies show to incorporate them into the life of the person wherever they are.

Such is the case of mobile devices or robotics, as discussed below.

One of the greatest efforts at present is made with respect to the treatment of Alzheimer's, seeking to slow the degenerative process until it stops.

Reversing the effects of Alzheimer's disease is as expected and desirable by researchers and family members of the patient, but when it comes to damaged structures, as in the case of neurons, it is very difficult to achieve recovery, despite which they ultimately seek the treatment for Alzheimer's.

Hence, drugs are being developed and exploring different types of treatments, such as genetic, in search of a "solution" that alleviates the progress of this disease.

Meanwhile, a series of neuropsychological techniques have been developed with which to compensate for the deficiencies that Alzheimer's disease progressively causes.

In recent years and thanks to the advancement and expansion of technology, programs or apps have been developed to automate some of the tasks performed with the neuropsychologist in neurorehabilitation.

And from other branches such as engineering, they

have tried to contribute their progress in improving the patient's quality of life, such as through robotics, which become true automated assistants that incorporate programs with which to stimulate Alzheimer's disease patients, but are robots good for Alzheimer's treatment?

This is what is sought from the Toronto Rehabilitation Institute, the University of Toronto (Canada) and the University of Massachusetts Lowell (USA), whose results were presented at the 5th Workshop of S.L.P.A.T. (Speech and Language Processing for Assistive Technologies) and published in the memoirs of that congress.

Ten adults over 55 years of age participated in the study, six of them women, all diagnosed with Alzheimer's disease. The participants received a tele assisted robot, with a built-in plasma screen where different messages oriented to the treatment of Alzheimer's appeared, these were small tasks that patients had to perform, common in neurorehabilitation. The instructions in addition to being read on the screen were read by the computer through a T.T.S. (Text-To-Speech).

An evaluation was carried out before and after the implantation of the robotic assistant to verify its effects on one of the factors affected by Alzheimer's such as language, specifically with regard to voice recognition. There was a significant increase in speech recognition of short and long sentences, extracted after an interview with both the patient and his caregiver.

Although the results are clear in terms of the benefits of using properly programmed robots, there is still a need to reduce the cost of these robots so that they can be available to any family member in order to extend Alzheimer's treatment to all those who need it.

CONCLUSIONS

The study of Psychology encompasses any human activity, to understand how this occurs and what influence this may have on your life, hence an increasingly frequent activity in both adults and young people is included, the use of widespread and intensive Internet especially regarding the use of social networks.

Aspect that in a short time has changed the way of "seeing the world" and interacting with others, opening up to new possibilities while taking care of the dangers of a network, such as cyberbullying or cyberaddiction.

In this e-book, the highlights of the incorporation of technology into the life of users from a psychological point of view have been addressed.

A novel perspective, which examines the role of the individual in this modern change, and how it transforms their way of thinking and their social relationships.

This is the first book in a collection that tries to explore in depth the influence of technology in the psychological world from different perspectives.

A theme so new that there are hardly any writings about it, this being the first book in the world published by a Spanish author about Cyberpsychology.

ABOUT JUAN MOISÉS DE LA SERNA

He is a Doctor of Psychology, Master in Neurosciences and Behavioral Biology, and Specialist in Clinical Hypnosis, recognized by the International Biographical Center (Cambridge - U.K.) as one of the one hundred best health professionals in the world of 2010. Developing his teachings in different national and international universities.

Scientific disseminator with participation in congresses, conferences and seminars; contributor to various newspapers, digital media and radio programs; Author of the blog "Open Chair of Psychology and Neurosciences" and seventeen books on various topics.

He is currently developing his research in the field of Big Data applied to Health, for which he works with data from India, USA. or Canada among others; work that complements with the advice to technological Startups oriented to Psychology and Personal Well-being.

www.ingramcontent.com/pod-product-compliance
Lightning Source LLC
LaVergne TN
LVHW052307060326
832902LV00021B/3756